To Addie, with much love.
From Náanii XOX
— K̲ung Jaadee

For my kids...always loved. ♥
— Carla Joseph

All text copyright © 2025 K̲ung Jaadee
All illustrations copyright © 2025 Carla Joseph

No part of this publication may be reproduced, stored or transmitted in any form—electronic, photocopying, scanning, recording, or otherwise—unless specifically authorized.
All rights reserved.

X̲aad Kíl/Haida Language Translator: Emily Edenshaw

ISBN: 9781778540639
Printed in PRC
Published in Canada by Medicine Wheel Publishing
www.medicinewheelpublishing.com

Medicine Wheel Publishing acknowledges that we live and work on the traditional and unceded lands of the Coast Salish People, including the T'Sou-ke People, the W̱SÁNEĆ People, the Sc'ianew People, and theləkʷəŋən Peoples.

I Am Connected

Kung Jaadee AND Carla Joseph

Medicine Wheel Publishing

I am connected to **myself**. I love myself. "I love me," I tell myself every day when I wake up and every night before I sleep.

Whenever I feel unwell, I **hug myself** tight as I remember my tens of thousands of ancestors who love me no matter what. **Who do you love?**

I am connected to my **ancestors**. I often make a spirit plate for them. I take a bit of food from each dish I make and set the plate beside mine.

I thank my ancestors for looking after me, then I eat my meal. You can make a spirit plate for your ancestors if you like. **What would you put on it?**

I am connected to the **earth**. I stand barefoot on the ground and feel the energy moving into my feet and body. I inhale deeply and smell the cedar, honeysuckle, spruce, and hemlock.

I feel the thick moss beneath my feet and notice the beautiful big ferns growing beside the huckleberry bush. I am thankful. **What are you thankful for?**

I am connected to **water**. I grew up on the ocean, as my dad is a fisherman. I need to be near the ocean every day so I can walk to the beach and wade in.

Sometimes I spend a long time building sandcastles beside the water and watch the ocean wash it all away. It's okay. I can build another one tomorrow.
What do you like to build?

I am connected to the **trees**.
For as long as I can remember,
I needed to climb trees.

I climb to the top of my favourite tree and look at the world from there. I am strong. **What do you do to feel strong?**

I am connected to the **ravens**. My mom taught me that we belong to the Raven Clan because my Náanii (grandmother) is Raven.

My dad belongs to the Eagle Clan because his mother is Eagle. When I go for walks, a raven flies overhead and calls out to me. I call back in response.
Have you ever tried talking to the birds?

I am connected to our **dormant volcano, Taaw Sdalee** (taw sdah-lay), or Tow Hill. I grew up climbing him from a young age, long before there was a trail leading people to the top.

On a clear day, we can see the mountains in Alaska.
Is there a favourite place you like to walk to? What do you notice along the way?

I am connected to **Haida Gwaii**, the Land of the People. My grandparents and I were born and raised here. My ancestors were born and raised here, too.

My mother moved here when she was almost grown up. Haida Gwaii, Dáng díi k̲uyáadaang. I love you, Haida Gwaii. **Where were you born?**

I am becoming connected to my **granddaughter**. I sing nursery rhymes to her in our language; I speak to her in X̱aad Kíl (Haida language).

I tell her, "Dáng án guudangaagang. You're so cute!"
And, "Dáng án dagwíiaagang. You're so strong!"
And, "Dáng án k'adangáagang. You're so smart!"
I am grateful to be a Náanii (a grandmother).
We are connected.

"Dáng án guudangaagang"
"Dáng án dagwíiaagang"
"Dáng án k'adangáagang"

The ancestors, Mother Earth, the trees, the animals, all people, you and me...

Photo credit: Kim Thé

Author

K̲ung Jaadee (Roberta Kennedy) is a professional Indigenous storyteller, educator (BA and BEd) and published author who has been telling stories for 30-plus years across Canada. She belongs to the X̲aayda (Haida), xʷməθkʷəy̓əm (Musqueam), Sk̲wx̲wú7mesh (Squamish), Tlingit, səlilwətaɬ (Tsleil-Waututh) Nations, and is also part Hawaiian. She was born and raised on Haida Gwaii and is from the Yaguu'laanaas Raven Clan. She now resides with her family in East Vancouver on the unceded traditional territories of the xʷməθkʷəy̓əm, Sk̲wx̲wú7mesh, and səlilwətaɬ Nations.

Her Haida name, K̲ung Jaadee, was presented to her at her great uncle's memorial feast by her cousin, Crystal Robinson, and means "Moon Woman." Her Aunt Leialoha gave her the name, Hi'ilawe, in reference to the most famous Hawaiian waterfall on the Big Island.

Over the past three decades, K̲ung Jaadee has performed traditional Haida legends, while also sharing vivid personal stories about her clan's survival of the smallpox epidemic, and the history and culture of her people. She is also the author of the popular children's books, *Raven's Feast* and *Gifts from Raven* (selected as a Local BC Book to Read), as well as the textbooks, *Haida Nation: Indigenous Communities in Canada* and *Haida Gwaii: We Are Home*. Her stories have also been published in several anthologies, magazines and online publications. In recent years, K̲ung Jaadee also worked as the Vancouver Public Library's Indigenous Storyteller in Residence.

Illustrator

Carla Joseph is a Métis/Cree artist born in Prince George, BC. Carla received her key to become an artist in residence at the Prince George Community Arts Council in 2016. She went on to win Art Battle in 2016 and 2018. Carla has her own very unique style which many people connect with. She loves the way she makes people feel with her art and it inspires her to continue with her gift. Carla loves to challenge herself by taking on many different projects that can be seen around her home community. Carla has illustrated at least five wonderful children's books, including *Be a Good Ancestor*. She now resides in the lower mainland.

Kung Jaadee is a professional storyteller, educator, and author with over three decades of experience. She has performed traditional legends and personal stories at hundreds of festivals, schools and Indigenous celebrations across Canada. Kung Jaadee states "storytelling chose her" and loves to share her gift of storytelling with people of all ages across Turtle Island.

Kung Jaadee's Storytelling and Keynote performances include:

* Haida Stories
* Squamish Stories
* ReconciliACTION Workshop
* Keynote Presentation—Haida history, stories and songs
* Virtual Haida Stories & Squamish Stories Programs

To book Kung Jaadee, visit:
pebblestarartists.com/kung-jaadee

Keep up to date with Kung Jaadee at:
 Storyteller Kung Jaadee
 @kungjaadee

Photos credit: Kim Thé